VELÁZQUEZ

The life and work of the artist illustrated with 80 colour plates

---

EMMA MICHELETTI

THAMES AND HUDSON

Translated from the Italian by Rosalind Hawkes

This edition © 1968 Thames and Hudson, 30-34 Bloomsbury Street, London WC1

Copyright © 1968 by Sadea Editore, Firenze

Printed in Italy

Life

Diego de Silva Velázquez, usually known by his mother's name, Velázquez, was born in Calle de la Móreira, Seville, in 1599, and baptized in the parish church of San Pedro on 6 June. His father, Don Juan Rodríguez de Silva y Rodríguez, was the son of a Portuguese *hidalgo*, who may have moved from Seville to Oporto in the mid-sixteenth century; his mother Jerónima Velázquez was from Seville. Like many young men from good families, he probably had a thorough literary education, and all his life kept up his faith in the world of culture, particularly the classical. His library was evidence of this: greatly superior to those of most painters of his time, it was rich in poetry, religion, medicine, engineering and mathematics, and especially in works by Aristotle, Horace, Ovid, Pliny, and by Ariosto, Castiglione, Vasari, Vesalio and Dürer. It seems clear that he developed a special interest in architectural treatises, from Vitruvius to Alberti, Scamozzi, Serlio, Palladio and Vignola. All this suggests that the young Velázquez had a good, rigorous and well-balanced formal education. Perhaps encouraged by his cultivated master, Francisco Pacheco, he formed his roots in the fundamental principles of the Italian Renaissance.

Velázquez felt his vocation to art very early: at the age of eleven, according to tradition, he joined the workshop of Francisco de Herrera the Elder, a painter of severe realism, which was the tendency in Spain at that time. Velázquez was apprenticed to Francisco Pacheco on 1 December 1610, and remained with him for six years. These were the most important years in his cultural and artistic formation; he owed much to the constant presence of his master (later his father-in-law), and to his environment in Seville, then closely identified with the new Italian painting.

In 1617 Velázquez was received into the guild of painters of St Luke, and obtained his diploma and credentials as an independent artist. On 23 April 1618 he married Juana

3

Miranda Pacheco, daughter of his master, who recorded in his *Arte de la pintura* that ' after five years of education and training I married him to my daughter '. The young painter already had many works to his credit, including mainly *bodegones*, genre scenes done from life in the market and taverns, a theme dear to Pacheco, who in some respects was a follower and admirer of Caravaggio. From this period also date the first portraits, those of Pacheco (*pl. 7*), the priest Suárez de Ribera, and, particularly significant, Mother Doña Jerónima de la Fuente (*pl. 6*) and religious paintings like the *Immaculate Conception*, in the Woodall Collection (on loan to the National Gallery, London), *St Paul, St Thomas* (*pls 2-3*) and *St John the Baptist* in Barcelona, Orleans and London respectively, and finally the *Adoration of the Magi* (*pls 4-5*) in the Prado.

As he grew more mature and his art developed, Velázquez became intolerant of the artistic environment round Pacheco, the ties with the Italian Renaissance tradition which seemed to him ultimately to consist only of a constricting system of measurements, formulae and rules for composition and equilibrium. However, Pacheco saw clearly how Velázquez's spirit shied away from the basic rules of art in which he himself believed. He realized the importance of broader contacts and urged him to visit Madrid, and especially to see the rich selection of Italian art to be found in the great royal collections. In 1622 Velázquez arrived in the Spanish capital for the first time. But as Pacheco wrote, everything was barred to him, and ' for the time being he found no way of painting the royal family despite his attempts ', so he returned to Seville. A year later, however, in 1623, he and his father-in-law were presented to the powerful Count-Duke Gaspar Guzman de Olivares, through the influence of Don Luís and Don Melchior de Alcazar, and notably of the Sevillian Don Juan de Fonseca, the king's chaplain, of whom he painted a portrait which was later much admired by the court. This marked the end of the Seville period and the painter's youth.

The doors of the court were opened to him, bringing the favour of the king, the goodwill of court circles, and the famous royal galleries. In August 1623 he painted his first portrait of the young king, Philip IV, after that of his patron, the Count-Duke Olivares. In September he painted the Prince of Wales, afterwards Charles I of England, when he was the guest of the Spanish court, and finally on 6 October he was made 'painter to the king' and officially received into the king's service. In 1624 he settled himself and his family in Calle de la Concepción, Madrid. His connection with the king ended only with his own death. If these conditions sometimes took away his freedom, they allowed him to live a peaceful life free of financial cares; for his part the sovereign did not weigh him down unduly with obligations and terms. He understood his painter, 'phlegmatic' by nature, as Philip IV said, and truly southern in spirit and character, and although commissioning many works from him left him free to work in peace, as he chose, agreeing also to not being his exclusive client. In 1627 Velázquez won a court competition, with a painting of *Philip III and the expulsion of the 'Moriscos' from Spain,* over other more senior court painters – Vicente Carducho, Eugenio Caxés and Angelo Nardi – and was made Usher of the Chamber. In September 1628 Rubens arrived in Madrid, and Velázquez accompanied the great Fleming on visits to the palaces and royal collections. It was Rubens who induced his new friend to visit Italy, and Velázquez set out at the beginning of August 1629, after he had painted the *Bacchus (pls 12-17)*, better known as *Los Borrachos (The Topers)*, some of the early portraits of Philip IV, and the Infante Don Carlos *(pls 10, 11)*, and other works.

Velázquez embarked at Barcelona on 10 August (St Lawrence's Day, as Pacheco noted), and reached Genoa on 20 August. Passing through Milan he went on to Venice, the city which appealed, more than any other in Italy, to his taste for colour, softness and glow in painting. From there he went on to Ferrara, Bologna, and Cento, where he especially admired the work of Guercino. After visiting Loreto he stayed a year in Rome and there came into contact with the Venetian neoclassicism of the Carracci, and the art of Pietro da Cortona, creator of the baroque taste in Italian painting. We can be certain that during this year he painted *Joseph's bloody coat brought to Jacob (pls 22-3), The*

5

Forge of Vulcan (*pls 18-21*), and the *Gamblers in a brawl* (*pls 24-5*) which has only recently been definitively attributed to him (Longhi). After Rome came Naples, the last and for a Spaniard almost obligatory stage, as it was considered an outpost of Iberia. Here he naturally met his compatriot José de Ribera, *il spagnoletto*, and painted the Infanta María of Bourbon, sister of 'his' king, travelling to her future husband, Ferdinand of Hungary. By January 1631 Velázquez was once more in Madrid.

At this point began his second period, lasting until his second Italian journey about eighteen years later. He painted many of his best-known works during this period, including the large equestrian portraits of the royal family (*pls 32-8*) and a second series as hunters (*pls 45-7*), the magnificent portrait of *Francesco II d'Este* (*pl. 52*), a guest at the court, and the many portraits of the palace dwarfs and buffoons: *Pablo de Vallalolid* (*pl. 30*), *Don Diego de Acedo* (*pl. 53*), *Sebastián de Morra* (*pl 55*), *Calabazas* (*pl. 54*), *Don Cristobal de Castañeda y Pernja* (*pl. 57*) and *Don Juan de Austria* (*pl. 56*). Some of his few religious paintings also belong to this period, such as the *Christ on the Cross* (*pl. 48*) from the Benedictine convent of San Plácido, now in the Prado, the *Christ after the Flagellation contemplated by the Christian soul* (*pls 28-9*) in London, the large *Coronation of the Virgin* (*pl. 59*) and the *St Anthony Abbot and St Paul the Hermit* (*pl. 51*). In 1633 he married his daughter Francisca to his pupil Juan Bautista del Mazo; at the same time he continued the decoration of the Hall of Realms at the Buen Retiro, which included the painting of *The Surrender of Breda* (*pls 39-44*). He was made Gentleman of the Wardrobe in 1634, and in 1643 Gentleman of the Bedchamber. In January 1649 he departed again for Italy, this time in an official capacity. He accompanied the Duque de Nájera, leader of the embassy, to Trent to receive the new queen, Mariana of Austria, and at the same time was entrusted by the king with acquiring works of art in Venice and Naples. He stayed over a year in Rome, and after exhibiting with great success a painting of his mulatto assistant Pareja in the Pantheon, he painted the brilliant portrait of *Pope Innocent* X (*pl. 62*).

Perhaps datable to this same year, 1650, are the two views of the *Villa Medici, in Rome* (*pls 63, 64*). Meanwhile he was nominated to the Academy of St Luke.

In 1651 he was recalled to Spain by the king who made him *Aposentador Mayor de Palacio* (Chamberlain of the Palace). He moved with his family into the so-called Treasure House adjoining the royal palace, but his new and far more exacting duties increasingly prevented him from devoting himself to painting. These were painful years too in his personal life, just as they were harder and sadder for the Spanish throne and for Iberian power. His father-in-law and his daughter Francisca both died in 1654. In 1658 the king bestowed on him the greatest honour in Spain, the Order of Santiago, which was granted to him as an 'honest, legitimate son, a Christian without fault' but above all because he practised his own art 'as an honourable pastime'.

Velázquez left Madrid on 8 April 1660 for Fuenterrabia to decorate the rooms in a palace on the Isle of Pheasants, in the river Bidassoa, where the Infanta María Teresa was to be ceremonially presented to her future husband Louis XIV. After returning to Madrid, the painter caught a severe fever on 26 June, and died on 6 August. His most famous works belong to the last years of his life: *Venus at her mirror* (*pls 66-7*), *The Royal Family* (*pls 77-9*), *The Fable of Arachne* (*pls 74-6*), and the many magnificent portraits of Philip IV, the young Queen Mariana (*pl. 71*), and the charming and vivacious little Infanta Margarita (*pl. 73*).

Works

Velázquez's life was decidedly a successful one, and in some respects a parallel with Rubens almost instinctively comes to mind. They were, as we have seen, close friends. Both were born in the month of June; both seem to have found in this glowing summer month the auspices of an easy and contented life and an early, assured and illustrious artistic achievement; both were in the service of understanding and generous sovereigns whom they served faithfully and with affection; both died while still active, just over sixty years old, at the summit of their artistic careers, when indeed little could have been added to perfect their style and technique. They differed in spirit, in their expressive and emotional strength, and in character; Rubens was powerfully alive, direct and extravert, while Velázquez was calm, reflective and a careful observer.

In the work of his prime and of the end of his life, Velázquez is undoubtedly *il pittore* – ' the painter ' in the most complete and perfect sense of the term. He perceived and assimilated every object and re-expressed it in a lustrous glow of colour. Everything he looked at he turned into poetry, and every image took on a poetry of its own, never distorted or idealized. He was careful of every detail, observing the reality of the object, and especially of the human figure, in conformity with the general tendency in Spanish art in his time. But it was certainly his painting which marked the definitive break with what remained of the influence of the sixteenth century. Before reaching this detailed vision of the world, of nature, men and things, Velázquez had acquired a vast range of professional experience, and by his journeys and contacts he developed a profound knowledge of Italian and, to a lesser extent, Spanish painting.

As we have seen, he began his career in the studio of Francisco Pacheco, who, though somewhat lacking in imagination, possessed thorough technical ability, and was an admirer of the great Italian painters of the Cinquecento, particularly Raphael. Velázquez followed the strict formal rules of this painter, yet soon turned in another direction, towards a closer observation of the common objects and figures of everyday life. Seville, the place in which he worked, was the Spanish city most closely identified with avant-garde Italian culture, as represented by the second wave of Caravaggesque genre scenes of interiors of taverns and workshops. These the young Velázquez made his own, and became the finest exponent of the type outside Italy. It was a calling that he felt so strongly in himself and for his own life that he readily chose the simplest and lowliest of material objects to paint: fish left in a basket, pans and pitchers in the semi-darkness of a kitchen, a white table-cloth bright in the smoky shadows of a tavern, an egg frying in a pan (*pl. 1*). Sharing the existence of these poor and trivial objects is a race of simple human beings, some-times disagreeable in aspect, but real in pose and gesture, real in the lifelike network of wrinkles on a face or in the flash of a sudden smile on rough, sturdy peasant features. All these are found in the tavern scenes (*bodegones*) now to be seen in Leningrad and Budapest, in the *Waterseller* in London, and the servant girl in the *Christ at Emmaus* now near Dublin.

Furthermore, his attempt to unite the foreground with the distance, principally by the use of light, is clearly visible in these works; we will find this problem perfectly resolved at the end of his life in *The Fable of Arachne.*

After only a few years of his working life, it was already obvious that the portrait was the type of painting most congenial to him, even though he also painted religious pictures, historical and mythological scenes, interiors and landscapes. Despite his limited output (about a hundred and twenty paintings are known), Velázquez undoubtedly tack-led problems of every type, dealing with a great variety of subjects. He was less productive in the religious paint-ing which was typical of every other painter of his time, although paintings of this kind constantly recur throughout his life's work. Observation of the individual interested him more. It was the infinite variety of mankind that always especially attracted him. His technique developed and became more fluid; his use of colour moved away from the dark, sombre, bituminous tones, with sudden flashes of glowing light, which are characteristic of the Seville period, and turned softer and clearer, never too vivid, to an unforgettable range of silvers, pinks, blues, mauves and blacks bathed in a pale, calm and restful light.

In the *Adoration of the Magi* (*pls 4-5*) of 1619, he had already painted his young wife, his father-in-law Pacheco, and daughter Francisca, born that year. The scene is simply composed and still typified by the very strong contrast of chiaroscuro, and by the usual sombre colour of this period, but it is understood mainly as an ordinary scene of everyday life in which a group of adults, each one an individual, is gathered round a new-born child who is, logically, the psychological centre of the composition. The ' portraits ' of *St Thomas* (*pls 2-3*) and *St John the Baptist* in the National Gallery, London, and *St Paul* in Barcelona, are characterized by assurance and precision in the physical features, pose and setting.

These paintings are very similar to the most significant work of this period, the portrait of *Mother Doña Jerónima de la Fuente* (*pl. 6*). The dark mysterious mass of her form and the severe, withered, and deeply furrowed face, undoubtedly put it close to Velázquez's topers, customers of the *bodegones* (low eating places), as a product of Velázquez's search for truth and concreteness. Here indeed the artist gained his first major success; this is an enquiry in paint into the character of an extremely determined woman, a nun from Toledo who had left her convent at an advanced age to embark at Seville on her way to the Philippines. Even then, at the age of twenty, Velázquez seemed to have reached maturity. The Seville paintings clearly show the direction he chose to follow, that of naturalism. He is beginning to attain this in his mastery of vigorous drawing, decisive modelling, and a chiaroscuro which emphasizes light and form.

However, Velázquez was soon concerned with new interests, and Seville no longer satisfied him. Pacheco himself sensed the need for new encounters and fresh experience for his son-in-law, now an independent artist. It was the road to Madrid which now assumed importance, not so much for its artistic environment, which may have been narrower and more rigidly Spanish than in Seville, but for its rich selection of paintings enclosed in the royal collections of the Alcazar, and necessary for his complete formation as an artist. But on his first visit there in 1622 he drew a blank. The Alcazar remained closed to him; he naturally looked at the work of El Greco with fresh wonder and interest. El Greco had died in 1614, and his shadow dominated the entire artistic environment in Madrid. Back in Seville, Velázquez must have felt that he could only live there temporarily, and then at last he was called back to Madrid by the powerful Count-Duke Olivares, this time for ever.

He was welcomed to the court where the young sovereign, gloomy and weak-willed, seemed to want to recapture, in the Alcazar, the Torre de la Parada and the Buen Retiro, the magnificence of Charles V. The Spanish monarchy was passing the peak of its remarkable concentration of political power – a period during which Spain had dominated the European world.

In 1623 Velázquez, now completely formed as a painter, came into direct contact for the first time with Italian art of the Cinquecento. In the paintings of the royal collections he discovered the Venetians, becoming absorbed in Titian's intense glow and range of colour. At the same time he became fascinated by the calm, grey tones of El Greco's colour. His art developed steadily and peacefully without sudden discordant changes or *volte-faces*, because he had the gift of remaining always true to himself. He softened his drawing style and relaxed his previous formal stiffness; his composition became less stiff; he seemed to be trying out lighter colours which were calmer and more tranquil. This development was so gradual that the transition from the severe figure of *Mother Doña Jerónima de la Fuente* to the portrait of the *Infante Don Carlos* (*pl. 10*), and the early ones of the young king, seems effortless. Velázquez was still using dark colours not very different from those of the Seville period, but he was already experimenting with softer tones. Meanwhile he was adapting himself easily to his new position of king's painter. It has been said that the real history of Rubens began after his journey to Italy: in the same way it can be said that the art of Velázquez essentially began with his arrival in Madrid, especially when the Alcazar was opened to him. He established himself at the Spanish court as a portrait painter first of all, and the portrait of his patron Juan de Fonseca, now lost, served as an introduction to the king.

Henceforward his models changed. No longer were they the common people, drinkers and traders, but royalty, great dignitaries, and court buffoons. He approached them with just the same care and affection which he brought to all his subjects, and his portraits remained ideal and imaginative renderings. We find this in the so-called *Self-portrait* (*pl. 9*), which some modern critics identify as a portrait of his brother Juan, and more strongly in the large portrait of *Philip IV* (*pl. 11*), the first of the many portraits of the king painted by Velázquez. His first awareness of Titian's range of colour is expressed in this portrait, in the glowing play of the blacks, sometimes sombre, sometimes vivid; and in all the fluctuations of the intensity of the light before it floods over the golden floor on which the king's shadow falls, less dense than its figure, to form a muted comment on the whole composition. Many portraits followed, of the sovereign, the Infante Don Carlos, and Count-Duke Olivares, whose imposing array of decorations, cloak and military posture are an accurate reflection of his immense power over the young king. There were other portraits too of unknown persons, some melancholy, like the young man in the portrait in Munich (*pl. 8*), some unfinished or unpleasant, like the deformed gentleman in Detroit, some keenly alive like the *Geographer* in Rouen, known also as *Democritus* and as *Christopher Columbus*.

Velázquez also painted for the king a mythological scene, *Bacchus* (*pls 12-17*), which was paid for in 1629, according to the list of the king's own payments of 22 July, ' for a picture of Bacchus that he has done on my service '. Velázquez here tackled the Olympian gods for the first time, but he did so in a spirit very different from Titian or Rubens. He looked at the world of the gods with the same directness and freshness of vision which he had brought to the characters of the people of the streets and markets in his Seville period. The work, which is now in the Prado, and better known as *The Topers* (*Los Borrachos*) than by its correct name, reinterprets Titian in a very naturalistic key. It shows a group of lively men in rags and shabby hats, elated with wine, restricted and unsteady in the wavering movements of heads, hands and drinking-cups, their eyes winking and sparkling, and with somewhat stupefied smiles on their faces. Close by them are the semi-nude figures of Bacchus and his companions, their heads wreathed in vine leaves and bunches of grapes. The work is again similar to the tavern scenes in Seville in the figure types, colours and chiaroscuro. Rubens was staying in Madrid in 1628, and it was perhaps his lively presence, and his intense sensuousness and feeling for humanity, which influenced the young Velázquez when he returned to the manner of his recent past to depict a mankind very much of flesh and bone, transforming even gods into roisterers.

It was the daily meetings with Rubens, a guest of the Spanish court, which persuaded him to make his first Italian journey in 1630. This was a fundamental turning-point in his artistic life, as he renewed his acquaintance with Italian art, again particularly with the great Venetians of the sixteenth century with whom he felt the greatest sympathy, with the Venetian neoclassicism of the Carracci, and with the realistic and amusing world of the *bamboccianti* and their representation of landscape. On the other hand, Velázquez's presence in Italy was almost as important for the Italian, especially Neapolitan, artists; he represented a stronger and more solid faith in truthfulness to nature.

He stayed a year in Rome as a guest at the Villa Medici, and painted at least three works, which revealed a new and decisive turning-point in his art, *The Forge of Vulcan*, *Joseph's bloody coat brought to Jacob*, and *Gamblers in a brawl*.

13

In *The Forge of Vulcan* (*pls 18-21*) he is concerned with the Olympian gods again, but expresses the theme with a fresher and more immediate perception. Certainly for Velázquez ' the mythological world did not transcend . . ., it was something inherent in the reality of daily life '. With a few exceptions, his religious paintings show the same conception. There is indeed some reference to classical beauty in this work, in the half-naked Apollo wrapped in his robe of a soft golden colour, but this contrasts with the rough realism of the smiths at their work, and the anger of Vulcan at the disclosure of Venus' treachery, which summarize and clearly express individual characters. Velázquez's style was now developing; his figures were set more freely and easily in space; he treated his subjects more pictorially and with less modelling; and his style was already hinting at his perception of new problems of spatial distance which would occupy him more fully on his return to Madrid.

The same development took place in the biblical scene (*pls 22-3*), *Joseph's bloody coat brought to Jacob*. The naked outlined shoulders of the two brothers are among the most powerfully real and perfect examples of figure painting in Spanish art. The composition, with all its freedom of movement, draws together the despair of the old man, the indifference of the onlookers, the irritable snarling puppy, and the bright patch of sky and landscape on the left.

The small *Gamblers in a brawl* (*pls 24-5*) in the Pallavicini collection can probably be dated to 1630. Perhaps Velázquez painted it for his own pleasure, as if shrugging off the encumbrance of his two previous commissions, one a mythological subject, the other biblical. The artist's watchful eye was everywhere, on the faces, clothing, muskets, and excited gestures as if he were relating an event taking place ' in the colour of the Roman air, hung over with cloud ' (Longhi). The brawlers are Italian and Spanish, and the incident happens in front of a guardroom, possibly that of the country residence of the Spanish Embassy where the ambassador Monterey sought relief from the Roman summer. Indeed in the distance the Lake of Albano and Castelgandolfo are clearly recognizable. Velázquez had not previously been concerned with representing landscape. Probably the direct contact with the *bamboccianti* in Rome, in particular with Pieter van Laer and Cerquozzi, inspired him to it. The extensive areas of landscape in the *Royal Boar Hunt*, the *View of Saragossa* (*pl 61*), and the impressive and realistic rendering of the Dutch plains in *The Surrender of Breda* (*pls 39-44*) can be justified only after these new experiments had been sketched out in *Gamblers in a brawl* and *Joseph's bloody coat*. Later, in the two views of the *Villa Medici in Rome* (*pls 63-4*), his vision became enriched with a special atmosphere, quivering with light and impressionistic in manner, which anticipated Corot and Manet.

In Naples, just before leaving for Spain, he painted the Spanish Infanta María (*pl. 26*) travelling to join her future husband Ferdinand of Hungary. He said farewell to Italy with a portrait in which his manner showed more refinement of drawing and more glowing colour, diffused in calm and peaceful light. While in Italy Velázquez had steeped himself profoundly in the spirit of Italian art, and from what he saw had derived that nobility of feeling which made his ' realism ' more delicate, refined and intellectual. Henceforward everything was soft, serene and rich, delicate light harmoniously painted in pearly half-tones. Everything that was vibrant with life in Italian art inspired him, and enriched his own works. Thus he repeated a century later the phenomenon of Cervantes, whose Spanish nature underwent a mental awakening through his acquaintance with the Italian literature of the sixteenth century, at that time unknown in a Spain which was still bound by the dogmatic fanaticism and conservatism of the Middle Ages.

The second period of Velázquez's career began when he returned to Madrid in January 1631. These eighteen years were probably the most fruitful of his working life, when he developed his most characteristic manner, as far removed from the severity of the Seville period as it is from the impressionistic epilogue of his last ten years. He produced sixty paintings in this period, more or less half

his entire work. The paintings included portraits, mythological subjects, and one historical work.

A few canvases of religious subjects belong to this period.
Velázquez painted the *Temptation of St Thomas Aquinas*,
for Orihuela Cathedral, a work remarkable for its sur-
prising rhythm, and the *Christ on the Cross* (*pl. 48*) for the
Benedictines of San Plácido, now in the Prado, in which
the naked loneliness of the dead Christ, shown in a tragic
nocturnal light, is highly impressive. The *Christ after the
Flagellation contemplated by the Christian soul* (*pls 28-9*)
was painted about 1632, perhaps for a private oratory.
The unusual subject, connected to the vision of St Bridget
of Sweden, was quite common in Spain, although very
much in contrast with the pietism widespread in Spanish
religious painting. Perhaps it is really for this reason that
it makes an impression, through the more lifelike Italian
realism of the forms, particularly the firm and classical
body of the scourged Christ, which is nevertheless suffused with a liquid, vibrant light, and which balances harmoniously with the anxious contemplation of the boy
representing the Christian soul.

Then in *c*. 1640 came the *St Anthony Abbot and St Paul
the Hermit* (*pl. 51*). In this work, in which several events
are unfolded in the same scene, Velázquez seemed to turn
strangely to iconographical motifs of an almost Gothic
sort, whose stylized nature was hardly in keeping with
the immediate physical realization of the figures and objects
of his normal manner. But the most important part of
the work is the landscape, which is spread over a large
area of the painting in a very harmonious fusion and
weaving together of blues and greens. Velázquez attained
this exceptionally subtle technique later on in other works.
He seemed to be recalling his Italian experiences in this
work more than in others, in particular the same subject
by Pinturicchio in the Borgia apartments in the Vatican.
Velázquez's last religious work was *The Coronation of the
Virgin* (*pl. 59*), probably his least original painting; he
seemed to be tied to the tradition of El Greco and Dürer
as if compelled by the subject matter and his cultural
background. Yet the colour is lucid, intense, suffused with

light and throbbing with strong chiaroscuro, and the execution perfect in arrangement and composition.

Velázquez's sense of the dignity and importance of individual personality reached its climax in *The Surrender of Breda* (*pls 39-44*), one of the best-known of his paintings. It was painted in April 1635 and had historical precedent in a play by Pedro Calderón de la Barca, written ten years before and naturally known by Velázquez. It was Velázquez's only historical painting, and commemorated one of the most glorious moments in the history of Spanish power, which was decreasing, under a series of adverse blows of fortune, throughout the years when Velázquez was at the zenith of his artistic achievement. The painter tackled this new subject with balanced ease, reminding himself and perhaps others of his *Gamblers in a brawl* painted in Rome five years earlier. The work was soon popularly renamed *Las Lanzas* (*The Lances*), because of the verticals which seemed to express the peaceful halt of the army at the moment of surrender. It has been considered the best historical work in European painting. The victory of Ambrogio Spinola over the Dutch under Justin of Nassau is represented with no undue exaggeration, eloquence, or allegorical aid. Velázquez makes the distinctions between the various physical types of Spaniards and Dutch with great perspicacity. The land and sea of Holland is recognizable; Spinola, who travelled to Italy with Velázquez, may have described the scene to him in such detail that it could immediately be re-expressed in his mind and on the canvas. The colours are rich and pure, though not blaring or discordant, and blend together in the light midday air. The drawing is superlative, and the natural ease of the two opposing generals, the sorrowful dignity of the loser and the courteous smile of the victor, are extraordinary. This work can be considered a successful synthesis of the balanced maturity which Velázquez had attained at the age of thirty-six.

But it was in these eighteen years especially that he painted more and more portraits of the king, his family, guests and court buffoons. The series was diverse in character and expression, lacking only that pitiless introspection and

17

powerful irony that was to be typical of Goya. The equestrian portraits of the royal family, intended for the Hall of Realms at the Buen Retiro, were painted up to 1635. The great horses rear in baroque fashion and are set *en plein air* against glowing, airy landscapes which are barely outlined but are rich in atmosphere. The most beautiful of this series is clearly *Prince Baltasar Carlos (pls 33-4)*, which, like the other portraits, is set against the background of the Guadarra mountains. The boy's delicate face is painted in brief but essential half-tones, which, when looked at closely, seem almost to disappear in the vibrant air. The tranquil tones of the black, yellow, pink and white clothing blend agreeably against the clear blue of the sky. It is a light, airy, fragile painting, in which the modelling has become gentle, suffused with light, without the contrast of shaded areas.

Close to this is that of the king *(pl. 32)*, made almost monumental by his commanding pose, yet kept gentle by the gradual fading of the colour into the slightly clouded sky of the background. The portrait of Queen Isabel *(pl. 38)* is hard and more heraldic, perhaps partly owing to workshop assistance, but her face is magnificent, and the white horse very impressive, surely one of the most lifelike animals in all baroque painting. There were other official portraits in which the courtly elegance and traditionalism of the settings were substantially transformed into a fully modern style, as in the series of hunters painted from 1635 to 1640 for the hunting lodge called Torre de la Parada. One of these, the delicate likeness of Baltasar Carlos *(pl. 45)*, a little bigger now, is in the same airy, coloured atmosphere of calm and harmonious tones, while Velázquez's observant eye has lingered on the drowsy mass of the large dog lying near the boy's feet, bored by the long wait.

Also painted in these years were the portraits of the king's illustrious guests, like the very lovely one of Prince Francesco II d'Este *(pl. 52)*, done a little after the equestrian portraits of the Spanish royal family and *The Surrender of Breda*. The posture of the bust is firm and bold, and the red cloak wrapped round him enlivens the rather dark tones of the colours, which Velázquez's introspection seems to be making deeper, as if searching out the Machiavellian spirit of the Italian prince. The fairly bold colour range, based on the brown of the background, the silver of the armour, and the bright lustre of the great sash, is presented with deep atmospheric lightness, and is clearly Venetian in feeling, but expressed with greater strength and restraint. Other portraits of unknown persons include the *Woman as a Sibyl* (*pl. 27*), which many have sought to identify with Velázquez's wife Juanita Pacheco, and the other very beautiful unknown woman in the Wallace Collection, London, *Lady with a fan*, perhaps the painter's daughter Francisca.

But in the rooms of the Alcazar Velázquez did not study and paint only princes; he appeared to be fascinated by the strange world of buffoons, dwarfs and idiots who lived in the palace in daily contact with the king and princes. It was characteristic of the court of Spain, Don Quixote's own land, to have this collection of mysterious, deformed beings who were insane or retarded. Velázquez observed them because the endless variety of all mankind appealed to him, and he regarded this sad and degraded group of humanity, not maliciously, but rather with the respect which is due to every human individual. His paintings of them echo his respect, in the delicately fused and softened drawing, lacking the crude realism of the Flemish manner which would only have made soulless monsters of them. Something of the soul comes through in the shifting and vacant expressions on the poor wasted faces of these dwarfs. The first of the series, *Pablo de Valladolid* (*pl. 30*), otherwise known as *Pablillos*, may have suggested the idea of the *Fifer* to Manet. The dwarf is a figure in an atmosphere of receding space where everything flows together and fades without strength or substance. *Calabazas* (*pl. 54*), wrongly called *El bobo de Coria* (*The Half-wit of Coria*), expresses in his vague smile, perhaps more than any other, a feeble, docile and bewildered human being lost in the clouds of his madness. In spite of the elegance of his dress with its wide lace collar, his misfortune seems to be pointed to in the objects scattered around him, a

19

bottle or two, a glass, very different from the solid objects of the Seville period. Then came *Don Diego de Acedo*, ' *El Primo*' (*pl. 53*), whose physical misfortune may not have affected his mind, if it is true that he carried out administrative duties, as the large books and ink-well may have been intended to show. Yet the same sadness is passed on from the man's solemn and thoughtful face to his body, weaker and smaller than that of a child. Another dwarf was *Sebastián de Morra* (*pl. 55*), suspicious and introspective, his ridiculous limbs awkwardly and with difficulty supporting a huge head, surely full of crazed notions. *Don Juan de Austria* (*pl. 56*), bigger than Sebastián, is more sumptuously clothed, and surrounded, who knows why, by a breastplate, helmet and musket lying around his feet. Less unfortunate than the others was the buffoon *Don Cristobal de Castañeda y Pernja* (*pl. 57*), called Barbarossa, whose portrait, perhaps unfinished, is vivid with the bright colour of his red costume and full yellow cloak, and forms a huge, vibrant mass against the undefined gloom of the background.

Another series besides the fools is that of the hunt. There are more figures in movement; and the landscape is brought to life, by being represented with close adherence to nature, specifying very obviously every tree, every winding path, and every break in the ground, which is shown with that vital force later to reach full expression in Constable's work. In the hunting scenes animals appear: again horses and dogs of every kind, in every action, studied from life, with attention and faithfulness to their actual appearance in nature. Stags are included too, such as the superb *Head of a stag* in the Baiguer collection in Madrid, which must be ' the most splendid portrayal of an animal ever painted '. The landscape areas of the *Royal Boar Hunt* at once bring to mind the *View of Saragossa* (*pls 60-1*), painted during his stay in that city with the young Infante Baltasar Carlos in 1647. Although the work was signed by Juan Bautista del Mazo, Velázquez's son-in-law and apprentice, it has been considered at least the result of collaboration. Velázquez's contribution is shown particularly in the clean, curving outlines of the architecture, and in the use of small dabs of colour to bring the figures to life, reflected as they are in the green water with that realistic precision which was later to be characteristic of Guardi and Corot.

But it was always the portrait which urged itself on Velázquez, portraits of every type and individual in that infinite variety of humanity which his penetrating eye captured and accurately, though generously, observed. The portraits are so real and lifelike that they almost seem to breathe, even those of the two wandering philosophers, *Aesop* (*pl. 50*), and *Menippus* (*pl. 49*), painted for the decoration of the Torre de la Parada, as if in contrast to the sumptuous scenes by Rubens taken from Ovid's *Metamorphoses*. Both, the spiritualist and the cynic, look out at the world with disillusioned smiles, and seem detached from life, 'beyond good and evil'. More than any other work of this period, these best illustrate the development of Velázquez's art; even the objects painted at their feet – books, bowls, and jugs – are entirely different from those of his early years in Seville. A barely perceptible range of misty colour renders the objects almost incorporeal; objects which previously were represented as solid and completely real are now hardly more than suggested.

Included among the portraits is a representation of *Mars* (*pl. 58*) in the form of a half-naked man. His face, with its long black moustache, is partly hidden in the shadow of his helmet; his body has nothing of classical beauty, but rather the coarse realism of the roughest of the king's soldiers. It is perhaps the coldest and most academic of Velázquez's works, and seems almost to anticipate Ingres. He seems to have found difficulty in harmonizing the cold tone of the blue with the hot red colour.

Venus at her mirror (*pls 66-7*) succeeds as a creative work in a very different way. This is variously dated between 1648 and 1651, but was perhaps painted by Velázquez just before he left for Italy. With complete frankness the painter attempted here, for the only time in his life and with astonishing results, the female nude, treating the subject naturally, with immediacy, and with infinite delicacy and modesty. Italian influence is easily discernible in this painting, Venetian in particular, but no individual name springs to mind, not even that of Titian or Giorgione. It is certainly less rich in its range of colour, less luscious, and less sensuous. The pose is easy and natural, although decidedly baroque, and it is definitely, with Goya's *Maja nude*, the most important female nude in the whole of Spanish painting.

Almost twenty years had passed since Velázquez's return to Madrid in 1631, and Spain and her king could no longer enjoy the optimistic calm of the 1630s. Sorrow and defeat weighed upon the country and the court: the French invasion in the east, the fall of the Count-Duke Olivares, the death of the queen and, prematurely, of the crown prince. But Velázquez's painting continued its slow, impassive development. He continued to work faithfully in the service of the king, seeming indeed to give close study to every brushstroke, until 1649, the date of his new journey to Italy. If the first journey to Italy had served as a ' finishing course ', mainly to increase his acquaintance with Venetian painting in Venice and Rome, and to gain a deeper knowledge of the Renaissance and the early seventeenth century, the second gave the proof that he was a great painter of whom Italy was still unaware. This proof came with the portrait of his mulatto assistant Pareja, shown with great success in the Pantheon, and with the yet greater *Pope Innocent X* (*pl. 62*).

The two portraits caused a great sensation in the city, rich though it was in art, artists, and glories of the more or less recent past. Velázquez's portrait was certainly something quite new, almost revolutionary, and it set up unchallengeable conditions for a true pictorial realism in which the artist expressed what he saw without pretence or deceit, freeing himself from the ' beautiful manner ', and grasping and recording all the human emotions of a living face. When Innocent X sat for him, there occurred one of the key turning-points in the art of the century. The brief audience, and very brief sitting, which the pope allowed the painter, were enough for him to gain a clear perception of his model, who remains in the portrait the close, taciturn and irritable old man who appeared to Velázquez's eye;

the severe head is shown with a stark truth reminiscent of Bernini's bust, although rather less benevolent. This extraordinary work seems to have been painted at a single burst, the direct consequence of a sudden brilliant inspiration; the model is not in a set pose, but seems to be resting in a chair for a moment during the day.

The unostentatious and almost anti-historical attitude revealed in this painting revolutionized the forms and systems of representation dear to the sixteenth century. Everything in it is new, but specially remarkable is the bold and subtle arrangement of the pictorial scheme, which is set in a masterly play of colour between the successfully harmonizing red and white, thus causing the light to be fragmented in an uneven glow. The amazing quality of the work at once struck the pope himself, who, torn between complaisance and rebuke, said it was 'too real'.

The two views of the *Villa Medici in Rome*, (*pls 63, 64*) are to be placed at this same time, because they reflect the same sensitive use of colour and mood, although some critics have held them to be earlier, ascribable to the painter's first stay in Rome. In 1909 von Loga, after extensive research, placed them more logically in 1650, because of the free, light brushstrokes, just as in the portrait of Innocent X and henceforward in all Velázquez's last paintings. These are almost impressionistic studies, but in them the treatment of light has been fully worked out and dealt with, a decisive factor in the artist's work after 1650. When he was in the gardens of the Villa Medici, with its tall, dark cypresses and noble Renaissance architecture, Velázquez seems to have felt the need to express enjoyment in an extremely direct manner, interpreting through his brush and his senses 'the glory of the Roman sun and the pearly light caressing the pagan statue'.

The titles *Mid-day* and *Evening*, given them by Lafuente Ferrari, are wholly appropriate; these two memories of landscape and time have a modern quality which recalls Corot to mind. And it is impossible to believe that a young man of thirty, Velázquez's age during his first Italian journey, could have reached the artistic maturity revealed in the two works, quite different in technique and feeling

23

from his other work of that time. Returning to Rome, he must have visited the Villa Medici again and have felt, passionately, the poetry of the place and the moment. His way of painting seems almost like an echo of a distant moment in time, retrieved and seen again with a more complete and matured sensitivity.

Already the last glorious works of Velázquez were being prepared, those which paved the way for the triumphs of modern representational painting. It was a definitive part of his work that his delicacy in handling light and atmosphere brought out a particular emphasis on pure form, constantly developing it even sometimes with some distortion. It was really Velázquez's last period, usually thought to begin with his return to Madrid in 1651, that had the greatest significance in two ways, poetic and technical. He returned to Spain in June, once more in the service of the king, and for him painted almost all his last works, though the actual number painted in this last decade was not in fact very great. They were again portraits, and very beautiful ones, mainly of the king but also of *The Infanta María Teresa* (*pl. 72*), the future queen of France, *The Infanta Margarita* (*pl. 73*), who died as Empress of Austria, the tiny Prince Felipe Prospero, the new queen Mariana, and other figures of the court such as the *Conde de Benavente* (*pl. 65*) or *A dwarf with a dog* (*pl. 70*). The king appears old and sad, his last illusions gone, and seeks to conceal even his final disappointments under the ceremonious severity of his detached and rigid air. The portraits of Philip IV, from those as a young man to the latest ones, could form a chapter to themselves in the work of Velázquez, who painted his king affectionately all through his life. The transformation of the man can be followed year by year in these official and familiar likenesses, each one serious, deeply felt and expressed, despite the grand public poses. For the rest, the painter always took infinite pains to create the likenesses of the royal family, to give life to so many shadows: the brothers of the king, the long, thin and sad figure of Cardinal Infante Ferdinand, Don Carlos, a tragic memory of the king himself, his lovely sister María, then betrothed to the future Charles I of England and later wife to Ferdinand of Hungary, his first wife Isabel of Bourbon, daughter of Henry IV of France and Marie de Médicis. But it is principally for the royal children that the master's brush evokes a real and sincere affection. His treatment was never as subtle or as gay as in painting the little Baltasar Carlos with his open smiling face, or as later in the lively, fair and sweet little Margarita.

Almost all these royal figures disappeared: only Philip IV survived the sad years of national catastrophe. He established a second family, and it was Velázquez who transferred to paint these new hopes, and painted the young queen in his new style with exquisite taste. *Queen Mariana (pl. 71)*, peeping out from her absurd regal attire, would have appeared in the Prado portrait only as a stiff and fair puppet had she not been brought to life through Velázquez's use of harmonious and subdued colour, and his soft impressionistic handling of the brush, with its full liquid strokes and its short, sharp ones, which sometimes merge together and at others remain separate. This is hardly still a portrait; it is a pure painting, controlled by his colour values of silvery greys, reds, whites, pinks, in which every detail lives and moves by itself.

Then, after twenty years, Velázquez fondly painted the little *Infanta Margarita (pl. 73)*, who brought Baltasar Carlos' unforgotten sweetness once more to life. The painter attained his most glowing and successful effects in this fair little figure, whom he painted seven times wearing various dresses with their huge lacy skirts.

Velázquez also painted for Philip IV at this time several canvases of mythological subjects: *Psyche and Cupid, Venus and Adonis, Apollo flaying Marsyas, Mercury and Argus (pls 68-9)*. These were for the Hall of Mirrors in the Alcazar, and, except for *Mercury and Argus*, were destroyed in the fire of 1734. The surviving painting is perhaps an extra one, in which Velázquez seems to turn strangely for a moment to a certain gloominess, blended expertly now, however, with his miraculous impressionism. Argus' features, illuminated by a ray of light falling mainly on the hair, are scarcely distinguishable from the strong shadowy cave, but nevertheless vigorous life throbs from the resting figure which is reflected in the glowing sky in the background, in the darker form of the heifer, Io, and in Mercury creeping in the shadow.

So we come to Velázquez's last works, the greatest and most important, and in these he tackled all the problems which he had repeatedly attempted and partially solved during the course of his career. Never as in these had he achieved the fusion between the real and the ideal, and at this point he discovered, once and for all, what has been called ' form out of colour '. The two large canvases in the Prado, *The Royal Family* (*pls 77-9*) and *The Fable of Arachne* (*pls 74-6*), are compared and associated by the critics because both show the painter's final and extraordinary manner.

The Fable of Arachne is probably a little earlier, since it is still similar to the work preceding Velázquez's second Italian journey. Taking this similarity into account López-Rey has recently suggested a probable date of about 1649, but a later date, about 1653-4, immediately after Velázquez's return to Madrid, is more convincing. Most probably the scene conceals the sad myth of Minerva and Arachne, which links Velázquez with Cervantes, the poet of the deluded and suffering Don Quixote. The story is presented only by allusion, in a subtle and rather complex manner, with unexpected revelations such as the play of light, which is particularly bright and shining in the background where the figures on the tapestry representing the rape of Europa are confused, through the painter's caprice, with those of the apparently principal figures. The workers, in their other function – of realism – dominate the foreground, intent on their looms, observed from life by Velázquez, who in this way relates the fantastic theme of the myth to the level of daily life, according to his ' system of realism '. The scene on the tapestry was very probably copied from a painting by Titian, at that time still in the Alcazar collection; Velázquez invests the Venetian's work with a new awareness of glowing light, entirely his own, which is rich in modern qualities, and in lively cultural traditions which were to be the strongest basis for the art of Goya and Manet.

Velázquez's career ended with his most significant and important work: *The Royal Family* (*Las Meninas*). He painted a few more portraits of the little Infantes right at the end of his life, of Prince Felipe Prospero, and lastly one of the young Infanta Margarita, now in the Prado, which was done in the year of his death in 1660 and left unfinished; but *The Royal Family* was really the consummation of his career, painted at the end of the splendid curve of his artistic development and one of the most precious contributions to pictorial art the world has ever known.

It was at once considered his best work, and Palomino was the first to write of it, in 1724, in an accurate monograph which identifies all those portrayed and the half-empty, shadowy room as the painter's own studio in the royal palace, formerly, perhaps, the bedroom of the late Prince Baltasar Carlos. This work achieves all Velázquez's ultimate aesthetic aims, principally excelling in the handling of the problem of form and plastic solidity, and in the glowing range of colour.

The painting is a multiple portrait of the royal family and court, set in the king's own surroundings. The principal figure, with all the power of her mischievous charm, is the little Infanta Margarita, who has burst into Velázquez's studio, followed by her ladies, dwarfs, and dogs, in a flurry of skirts, cloaks and ribbons, while he was intent on painting the king and queen. The sovereigns are represented indirectly; only their images are visible, reflected in the mirror hung on the wall in the background, where two large mythological paintings, one by Rubens, the other by Jordaens, are also hung. Velázquez achieves here, more than ever before, an intimate and meditated whole, where light, space and colour are united in a synthesis so bold that the like had not been achieved since the time of Caravaggio. In *The Royal Family* he attained the ambition which he had had throughout his life: to paint figures ' in their setting ', to catch hold of and represent the most impalpable and intangible things, such as light, air, the distance between figures, the atmosphere itself, which assumes a pure, delicate, sunlike colouring, and gives a special tonal colour to faces, materials, and expressions.

He achieves, above all, vision in spatial depth, anticipating the problems the impressionists faced and solved two centuries later. This multiple portrait of the royal family had become, as he wanted, a family scene in his studio.

The painter, though detached from Margarita and her followers, and from us, enters naturally into the scene, and has interrupted his work and turned aside to put down on his canvas this more lively, real and excited group, in the manner agreeing with his principles, which had remained constant since the Seville days of the *Waterseller* and *Mother Doña Jerónima de la Fuente*. Here the canvas is no longer a mere surface or barrier to the spectator, it reaches out to us and we are confronted and approached as never before by these figures seen and painted largely my means of light, as if they were made of it.

It has been called a multiple portrait, correctly, because it portrays the Infanta Margarita, the rather indistinct sovereigns, the two maids-of-honour, the two dwarfs Mari-Barbola and Nicolas de Portosalo, and finally Velázquez himself, who stands calmly, still vigorous in appearance, yet gentle, in his relationship to the plump sweetness of the little Margarita. There are various self-portraits attributed to him, two in the Uffizi in Florence and one in the Museo Capitolino in Rome, but this is definitely the most real and reliable. Descriptions of the painter say he was handsome of figure and that his physical looks reflected his goodness; and indeed, in this painting, which has passed on his likeness to us very successfully, his gentle, sad and dreamy expression is seen as if it were a mirror of his spirit. Velázquez seems to be fusing himself more than ever with his own work, celebrating once more ' the return to nature, to a highly expressive nobility, to his own unrepeatable, wonderful and almost sacred observation of life, and the idealizing search for a structural and compositional harmony '. So the life and work of Diego Velázquez ends. From the beginning his art was concerned with the observation and representation of reality, and ultimately he achieved a pictorial technique, which is a perfect synthesis, very similar to the synthesis achieved by the impressionists two centuries later.

Velázquez and the Critics

Velázquez's painting was acclaimed in his own life-time, and this was certainly largely owing to the king's trust and confidence in him.

In the seventeenth century there was a chorus of unanimous praise for him, apart from the one discordant voice of Vicente Carducho, a court painter and his rival, who in his *Diálogos de la pintura* of 1633, particularly criticized Velázquez's style for its directness, realism and 'lack of care'. Two biographies especially bear witness to this general praise, one by Francisco Pacheco in his *Arte de la pintura* of 1649, and the other by Antonio Palomino in his *Museo Pittorico* of 1724. These two works can be considered the prime sources for the life and work of Velázquez; Pacheco was in almost continuous close contact with him from 1610 to 1654, and Palomino, born in 1655, five years before the painter's death, must have been able to collect information without difficulty from those who knew him. It was Palomino who was responsible for successful and still acceptable interpretations of some of the paintings.

In the seventeenth century, therefore, Velázquez was admired and regarded as the great painter *par excellence*, especially by Diego de Saavreda Fajardo and Baltasar Gracián, who praised his great naturalness and put him on a level with Zeuxis, Parrhasius, and Apelles or with Raphael and Titian. He was mentioned with great admiration also by Marco Boschini in his *Carta del navegar pittoresco* of 1660:

> *l'Ano mileseicento e cinquant'un*
> *Fu don Diego Velázquez gran sugeto*
> *Del catolico Re pitor perfeto . . .*

'In the year 1651 Don Diego Velázquez, great subject and perfect painter of the Catholic King . . .'.

All this warm praise turned Velázquez into the ostensible painter of every sombre interior which Spanish art was producing at that time, and gave a false idea of how much he had painted and hence of the quality of his art. Velázquez fell considerably in the estimation of eighteenth-century critics who for the most part came to prefer Murillo's complete, sometimes affected, sweetness. But in 1776 Anton Rafael Mengs, writing to Antonio Ponz, was of the firm opinion that *The Fable of Arachne* was ' painted in such a manner that the hand seemed to have no part in the execution, as if it had been painted entirely by will . . . '. But from then on, and until the romantic period, very little was published about Velázquez and his work, the only informative articles about him being by Eugenio de Ochoa and Federico de Madrazo. However, in 1848, in the middle of the Romantic period, an important work was published by Stirling Maxwell, the *Annals of the Artists of Spain*, which can be considered the basic stage of English criticism on Velázquez. This was followed in 1851 by Richard Ford's excellent monograph, *The Life of Diego Rodriguez de Silva y Velázquez*. Henceforward, during the second half of the century, the great painter from Seville was the subject of attention all over Europe, and in Madrid the bicentenary of his death was celebrated in 1860. But it was principally Carlo Justi, in 1888, who laid the foundations for genuine and exact research into Velázquez's work, commenting especially on his vigour, perception, delicacy and precision combined with his immense naturalness and exceptional power of representation. New studies on him began to appear, and the works of Velázquez became, as befitted the nineteenth century, a new science.

Indeed the critical study of Velázquez, particularly in these last few years, since the commemorative exhibition held in Madrid in 1960 for the tercentenary of his death, is one of the most fruitful of recent times. It boasts such well-known historians – mostly Spanish – as Muñoz, López-Rey, Lafuente Ferrari, Gaya Nuñoz. These write of the modern quality of his technique, his interpretation and poetic transformation of reality, and present an increasingly accurate and limited number of his works.

OUTLINE BIBLIOGRAPHY:

F. Pacheco, *Arte de la pintura, su antiguedad y grandezas,*
Seville 1649; A. Palomino, *El Parnaso Español pintoresco
laureando,* volume III of *Museo Pictorico Escala optica,*
Madrid 1724; W. Stirling, *Velázquez and his Works,*
London 1855; C. Berwick Curtis, *A descriptive and historical
catalogue of the Works of Diego de Silva Velázquez
and Bartolommé Esteban Murillo,* London 1883; G. Cru-
zada Villaamil, *Anales de la vida y de las obras de Diego
de Silva Velázquez,* Madrid 1885; C. Justi, *Velázquez und
sein Jahrhundert,* Bonn 1888 (Italian edition, Florence
1958); A. de Berruete, *Velázquez,* Paris 1898; ' Velázquez '
in *Klassiker der Kunst,* Dresden 1925; August Loebmann
Mayer, *Velázquez. A Catalogue Raisonné of the Pictures and
Drawings,* London 1936; A. Muñoz, *Velázquez,* Rome
1942; E. Lafuente Ferrari, *Velázquez,* London 1943;
L. P. Fargue, *Velázquez,* Paris 1946; E. de Gué Trapier, *Velázquez,* New York 1948; R. Longhi, ' Velázquez 1630:
La Rissa dell'Ambasciata di Spagna ', in *Paragon,* no. 1,
1950, pp. 28-34; B. de Pantorba, *La vida y la obra de
Velázquez,* Madrid 1955; K. Gerstenberg, *Diego Velázquez,*
Munich and Berlin 1957; J. Ortega y Gasset, *Velázquez,*
Madrid 1959; F. Sánchez Cantón, *Velázquez y ' lo clas-
sico ',* Madrid 1961; *Velázquez y lo velazqueño,* Catalogue
of the exhibition for the centenary of the painter's death,
Madrid 1961; X. De Salas, *Velázquez,* London 1962; J.
López-Rey, *Velázquez. A Catalogue Raisonné of his Oeuvre,
with an Introductory Study,* London 1963; F. Sánchez Cantón, ' Velázquez au Prado ', in *Revue française,* February
1963; *Encyclopedia of World Art,* article ' Velázquez ',
with full bibliography, London and New York 1966.

Notes on the Plates

1 Old woman frying eggs, 1628. Oil on canvas, 99×169 cm. Edinburgh, National Gallery of Scotland. The date was revealed when it was cleaned in 1957. The English painter David Wilkie bought the painting in Spain in the nineteenth century. It passed to the Robinson collection and at the end of the century into the Cook collection at Richmond. It was acquired by the Edinburgh museum in 1955.

2-3 St Thomas, 1619-20. Oil on canvas, 94×73 cm. Orleans, Musée des Beaux-Arts. This was painted during Velázquez's years in Seville. In 1925 Manuel Gómez Moreno attributed it to Velázquez's Seville period, and this has been accepted by Roberto Longhi, Adolfo Venturi and all the modern authorities.

4-5 The Adoration of the Magi, 1619. Oil on canvas, 204× 125 cm. Madrid, Prado. This was perhaps painted for the Jesuit Novitiates of San Luís, Seville. It remained for some time in the Escorial as a work of Zurbaran, but its attribution to Velázquez has not been questioned since 1819 when it went to the Prado.

6 Mother Doña Jerónima de la Fuente, 1620. Oil on canvas, 160×110 cm. Madrid, Prado. The painting is signed and dated: DIEGO VELÁZQUEZ F. 1620. The signature was discovered only in 1927, during an exhibition in Madrid. The work was bought by the state in 1942. A copy by the painter himself is in Madrid in the collection of Don Alejandro Fernandes de Araoz, and there is another, possibly a preparatory study, at Tissington Hall, in England, the property of Sir William Fitzherbert.

7 Portrait of Francisco Pacheco, c. 1620. Oil on canvas, 40×36 cm. Madrid, Prado. This is one of Velázquez's first portraits. By 1746 it was already part of the royal collection, wrongly attributed to Tintoretto. Since 1819 it has been in the Prado. Allende Salazar, in 1925, was the first to recognize the sitter as the painter's father-in-law, but López-Rey calls it merely *Portrait of a man with a goatee.*

8 Portrait of a young man, c. 1626. Oil on canvas, 89×69 cm. Munich, Alte Pinakothek. Unfinished. It was bought in Madrid in 1694 on behalf of the Elector Palatine John William, for his art gallery in Düsseldorf.

9 Self-portrait, c. 1621. Oil on canvas, 56×39 cm. Madrid, Prado. López-Rey calls it merely *Portrait of a young man.*

10 The Infante Don Carlos, c. 1627. Oil on canvas, 209×125 cm. Madrid, Prado. This is probably Velázquez's only portrait of the Infante, son of Philip III. It was saved from the fire in the Alcazar of 1734. In 1816 it was in the Academía de San Fernando, and eleven years later it went to the Prado.

11 Philip IV, c. 1625. Oil on canvas, 201×102 cm. Madrid, Prado. This is one of the most celebrated of Velázquez's works. by Velázquez before his first Italian journey.

12-17 Bacchus, 1628-9. Oil on canvas, 165×225 cm. Madrid, Prado. This is one of the most celebrated of Velázquez's works. It was painted at Madrid before he left for Italy, and was always part of the king's collection. It has been widely known since the 1820s as *Los Borrachos* (*The Topers*).

18-21 The Forge of Vulcan, 1630. Oil on canvas, 223×290 cm. Madrid, Prado. This was painted by Velázquez in Rome, together with *Joseph's bloody coat brought to Jacob* (*pls 22-3*), and has been in the Prado since 1819.

22-3 Joseph's bloody coat brought to Jacob, 1630. Oil on canvas, 223×250 cm. Madrid, El Escorial. The work was painted during Velázquez's first visit to Italy and was bought, with *The Forge of Vulcan* (*pls 18-21*), by Count-Duke Olivares as a present for the king. The sides of the painting may have been trimmed down, since the figures of Jacob and the half-naked youth at the extreme left are cut off.

24-5 Gamblers in a brawl, c. 1630. Oil on canvas, 28×39 cm. Rome, Palazzo Pallavicini. The work was attributed to Velázquez by Roberto Longhi ('Ultimi studi sul Caravaggio e la sua cerchia', in *Proporzioni*, 1943, pp. 34-62), who considered that it was painted during the painter's most Caravaggesque period, while on his first visit to Italy.

26 The Infanta Doña Maria, Queen of Hungary, 1630. Oil on canvas, 58×44 cm. Madrid, Prado. The portrait is of Philip IV's sister, born in 1606, and married to Ferdinand of Hungary in 1631. Pacheco states that on this occasion the artist painted the whole work himself. At Velázquez's death the painting was in his studio; in 1794 it was in the Arco Palace, and in 1808 in the Buen Retiro.

27 A woman as a Sibyl, 1631-2. Oil on canvas, 62×50 cm. Madrid, Prado. The softer, more fused pictorial style suggests that this was painted about 1632. Madrazo identified the young woman as Velázquez's wife, Juanita Pacheco.

28-9 Christ after the Flagellation contemplated by the Christian soul, 1631-2. Oil on canvas, 165×206 cm. London, National

Gallery. This was painted soon after his first Italian journey. López-Rey dates it to 1626-8. In its vigorous modelling it is very similar to *The Forge of Vulcan* and *Joseph's bloody coat.* Justi (*Velázquez e il suo secolo*, 1909), has reasonably compared the naked Christ with Michelangelo's statue in Santa Maria Sopra Minerva in Rome; other writers have noticed the obvious influence of Bolognese and Neapolitan art. The subject is based on the vision of St Bridget of Sweden. It was bought in Madrid in 1858 by Sir John Savile Lumley, and given by him to the National Gallery, London, in 1883.

30 Pablo de Valladolid, c. 1633. Oil on canvas, 209×123 cm. Madrid, Prado. The painting can be dated about 1633, on the grounds that Pablo de Valladolid was a buffoon at the Spanish court from 1632 to 1648. From the Buen Retiro it went to the Academía de San Fernando and in 1827 to the Prado.

31 Don Gaspar de Guzman, Conde de Olivares, Duque de San Lúcar la Mayor, equestrian, c. 1634-5. Oil on canvas, 313×239 cm. Madrid, Prado. This was probably painted in 1634, and belonged to the Count-Duke. Later it passed to his descendants and in the eighteenth century to the Marqués de la Enseñada, who sold it to King Charles III in 1769. It was in the Prado by 1819. There are many copies and versions of this work.

32 Philip IV, equestrian, c. 1634-5. Oil on canvas, 301×314 cm. Madrid, Prado. This, with the other equestrian portraits of the Spanish royal family, formed a series decorating the Hall of Realms of the Buen Retiro. Some of them, such as this and the next plate, were painted entirely by Velázquez, but others show clear signs of assistance. They were in the 1772 inventory of the New Palace, and since 1819 have been in the Prado. There are many copies of this portrait of Philip IV, among them one in the Palazzo Pitti, Florence, attributed to Juan Bautista del Mazo.

33-4 Prince Baltasar Carlos, equestrian, 1634-5. Oil on canvas, 209×173 cm. Madrid, Prado. See note to *pl. 32;* there are many copies of this portrait also.

35-7 Philip III, equestrian, c. 1628-9. Oil on canvas, 300×314 cm. Madrid, Prado. Philip III, son of Philip II and Anne of Austria, had died in 1621. The painting was begun by Velázquez and finished by an unidentified pupil during the master's first Italian journey.

38 Queen Isabel of Bourbon, equestrian, c. 1628-9. Oil on canvas, 310×314 cm. This is another of the series of equestrian portraits painted for the Hall of Realms of the Buen Retiro (see *pls 32, 33-4, 35-7*).

39-44 The Surrender of Breda, 1634-5. Oil on canvas, 307×367 cm. Madrid, Prado. This shows Ambrogio Spinola, commander of the

Spanish army, receiving, from the hands of the Dutch governor Justin of Nassau, the keys of the fortress of Breda, taken on 5 June 1625. The painting, with other historical works, was to decorate the Hall of Realms of the Buen Retiro. Since 1819 it has been in the Prado.

45   Prince Baltasar Carlos as a hunter with two dogs, 1635. Oil on canvas, 191×103 cm. Madrid, Prado. At the bottom the boy's age is written in Latin: ANNO AETATIS SUAE VI. He was six years old on 17 October 1635. This was one of the series of hunters painted to decorate the Torre de la Parada, the royal hunting lodge on the Pardo estate. In the mid-eighteenth century the canvas was moved to the New Palace in Madrid, and in 1819 it went to the Prado.

46   Philip IV as a hunter, c. 1635-6. Oil on canvas, 191×126 cm. Madrid, Prado. This was one of the series of *Hunters* painted by Velázquez between 1635 and 1636, to decorate the Torre de la .Parada. López-Rey dates it *c.* 1632-3. A copy of this portrait, but without the cap, by Juan Bautista del Mazo, is in the Louvre.

47   The Cardinal Infante Don Ferdinand as a hunter, c. 1632-3. Oil on canvas, 191×107 cm. Madrid, Prado. This was another of the series of *Hunters* (see *pls 45, 46*), and is the only portrait of this prince by Velázquez.

48   Christ on the Cross, c. 1635. Oil on canvas, 248×169 cm. Madrid, Prado. This so called *Cristo de San Plácido* was painted for the Benedictine convent of San Plácido in Madrid. López-Rey dates it *c.* 1631-2. It was bought by Manuel Godoy, favourite of Charles IV, at the beginning of the nineteenth century. In 1829 the Duque de San Fernando de Quiroga, who then owned it, gave it as a present to Ferdinand VII of Spain, who, in his turn, gave it to the Prado.

49   Menippus, c. 1640. Oil on canvas, 179×94 cm. Madrid, Prado. At the top left is written MOENIPPUS. The long narrow shape of this painting suggests it must have been placed, like the *Aesop*, on a wall between two windows. The two works were probably painted for the Torre de la Parada. Goya made two well-known etchings of them.

50   Aesop, c. 1640. Oil on canvas, 179×94 cm. Madrid, Prado. See note to *pl. 49*.

51   St Anthony Abbot and St Paul the Hermit, c. 1640. Oil on canvas, 257×188 cm. Madrid, Prado. The painting was originally semi-circular at the top, and there are still traces of the former shape. It was painted for the Ermita de San Pablo, at the Buen Retiro, probably in 1640. It may have been moved from there to the church of San Antonio, also adjoining the Buen Retiro, where it was on the inventory for 1701. It has been in the Prado since its foundation in 1819. Dürer's engravings of the two hermits and Pinturicchio's fresco in the Borgia apartments in the Vatican have been suggested as sources for this work. But it is more likely that Velázquez was inspired by Savoldo's painting of the same subject, which he certainly saw when he was in Venice.

52 Francesco II d'Este, Duke of Modena, 1638. Oil on canvas, 68×51 cm. Modena, Pinacoteca. Velázquez may have painted the duke of Modena in the autumn of 1638, when the duke was in Spain for a few weeks to be godfather to the Infanta María Teresa. According to Palomino, the painter received a magnificent gold chain from the duke as remuneration.

53 Don Diego de Acedo, ' El Primo ', 1644. Oil on canvas, 107×82 cm. Madrid, Prado. Don Diego de Acedo was the buffoon of the king's brother, the Cardinal Infante Ferdinando, from 1635 to 1660, and was also concerned with administrative affairs, symbolized by the book and ink-well. The painting was done at Fraga, and has been in the Prado since 1819. P. de Madrazo in 1872 was the first to identify the portrait.

54 Calabazas, c. 1637-9. Oil on canvas, 106×83 cm. Madrid, Prado. The young fool Juan Calabazas or Calabacellas was in the service of the king's brother from 1627. He died in 1639, so that even if the technique appears to belong to a later period, the painting cannot be dated after that year. It is referred to as the ' half-wit of Coria ' in an inventory of 1794, and has been in the Prado since 1819.

55 Sebastián de Morra, c. 1644. Oil on canvas, 106×81 cm. Madrid, Prado. The portrait is of another fool in the service of the Infante Ferdinando, whom he accompanied to Flanders. In 1643 he entered the retinue of Prince Baltasar Carlos, son of the king, and remained at the court after the young heir's death until his own death in 1649. The portrait was removed to the Prado from the royal collection in 1819.

56 Don Juan de Austria, c. 1650. Oil on canvas, 210×123 cm. Madrid, Prado. Velázquez probably painted the portrait of this buffoon for the Buen Retiro. His real name is unknown, while the style suggests a date towards the end of the 1640s.

57 Don Cristobal de Castañeda y Pernja, c. 1640. Oil on canvas, 198×121 cm. Madrid, Prado. The subject, Don Cristobal de Castañeda y Pernja, called Barbarossa, was another court buffoon. The portrait is unfinished and is datable to after 1640. It is listed for the first time in the 1704 inventory of the Buen Retiro, and since 1827 it has been in the Prado. Goya made an etching of it.

58 Mars, c. 1642-4. Oil on canvas, 179×95 cm. Madrid, Prado. This was possibly painted for the Torre de la Parada. It went to the Prado in 1827.

59 The Coronation of the Virgin, c. 1642. Oil on canvas, 176× 134 cm. Madrid, Prado. Velázquez painted this for the oratory of Queen Isabel, probably about 1642 (López-Rey dates it *c.* 1644). Jusepe Martínez, Velázquez's friend and pupil, had made a copy for Saragossa Cathedral by 1644. The painting has been in the Prado since 1819.

60-1 View of Saragossa, 1647. Oil on canvas, 181×331 cm. Madrid, Prado. The painting, dated 1647 and signed by Juan Bautista del Mazo, perhaps commemorated the visit of the King and Baltasar Carlos to the city a few years before the child's death. Despite the lack of documentary evidence (see López-Rey, p. 174), I follow Madrazo in believing this to be an authentic Velázquez, but it was clearly painted with the help and collaboration of his relative and pupil Mazo. The work was moved to the Prado in 1819 from the royal collection. X-ray photographs have shown that originally a group of the *Virgin supported by angels* was in the sky. A Goyaesque copy belongs to Luís Peres Jstué of Saragossa.

62 Pope Innocent X, 1650. Oil on canvas, 140×120 cm. Rome, Galleria Doria-Pamphili. The portrait, painted in Rome, is signed on the piece of paper held by the Pope in his left hand. The date 1650 is just legible below. It is one of the greatest and most famous of Velázquez's portraits, and has never left the Doria family collection. Many copies exist, of which one is in the Wellington Museum, Apsley House, London.

63 Villa Medici in Rome, 1650. Oil on canvas, 48×42 cm. Madrid, Prado. This is often called *Evening*, and with its companion piece called *Mid-day*, was probably painted in 1650 although López-Rey and others date it to 1630. They were both unusual examples of the master's work. They were mentioned in the inventory of the Alcazar in 1666, and have been in the Prado since 1819.

64 Villa Medici in Rome, 1650. Oil on canvas, 44×38 cm. Madrid, Prado. See note to *pl. 63*.

65 Conde de Benavente, 1648. Oil on canvas, 109×88 cm. Madrid, Prado. The portrait of Don Juan Francisco, Conde de Benavente (1584-1652) was probably painted in 1648, when he had already received the Order of the Golden Fleece; he is wearing the insignia here. The painting may have been bought by Queen Isabella Farnese in Seville in 1729, and it was listed in the palace inventory at La Granja in 1746 as 'Portrait of an unknown man by Titian'. In 1819 it went to the Prado as by Velázquez. A copy is in the collection of Vizconde de Baiguer, in Madrid.

66-7 Venus at her mirror, c. 1650. Oil on canvas, 122 × 177 cm. London, National Gallery. This was painted, probably before June 1651, for Don Gaspar Méndez de Haro Guzman, Marqués de Eliche. In a description of his house dated 1 June 1651, the work is specifically mentioned as 'a painting on canvas of a naked woman lying on a coverlet . . . looking at herself in a mirror held by a boy, by the hand of Velázquez'. It has generally been considered that the work was painted after the second Italian journey, as it reflects Michelangelo, Titian, Tintoretto and Paolo Veronese. In 1688 the work passed into the Alba collection, where it remained until 1802. It reached England in 1813, was bought by J. B. S. Morrey of Rokeby Hall, and was acquired by the National Gallery, London, in 1906.

68-9 Mercury and Argus, 1658. Oil on canvas, 127 × 248 cm. Madrid, Prado. This is the only remaining canvas of the four mythological scenes painted by Velázquez in 1658 (López-Rey: c. 1659) for the Hall of Mirrors in the Alcazar. The others were destroyed in the fire of 1734. It has been in the Prado since its foundation (1819).

70 A dwarf with a dog, after 1650. Oil on canvas, 142 × 107 cm. Madrid, Prado. This work, which could with difficulty be taken (as was long thought) to represent the buffoon Antonio, 'El Inglés', who died in 1617, has been considered by some to be the work of Juan Carreño de Miranda, or by Mazo, or at least a collaboration. López-Rey attributes it to 'a seventeenth-century *pasticheur*'. It is unfinished and was probably painted after Velázquez's second Italian journey. Since 1819 it had been in the Prado. A copy is in the Staatliche Museen, East Berlin.

71 Queen Mariana, 1652-4. Oil on canvas, 231 × 131 cm. Madrid, Prado. This, with its companion piece of King Philip IV in military dress, was painted between 1652 and 1654. It was in the Escorial before 1700, and was moved to the Prado in 1845. It is one of the most most skilful and natural of Velázquez's portraits of women. A copy, very likely done in his studio, is in the John and Mable Ringling Museum of Art, Sarasota, Florida.

72 The Infanta María Teresa, c. 1652. Oil on canvas, 73 × 61 cm. Paris, Louvre. The portrait was probably painted about 1652, perhaps as a study for the larger portrait now in the Kunsthistorisches Museum, Vienna; López-Rey considers it a workshop portrait.

73 The Infanta Margarita, c. 1654. Oil on canvas, 70 × 59 cm. Paris, Louvre. The little princess is here about three years old. Velázquez painted the portrait about 1654, and the king gave it to his sister Anne of Austria, wife of Louis XIII of France. López-Rey considers it a workshop portrait.

74-6 The Fable of Arachne, c. 1653-4. Oil on canvas, 220 × 289 cm. Madrid, Prado. It was Angelo Iniguez who identified the subject as the myth of Minerva and Arachne. In the nineteenth century and for part of the twentieth the scene was thought to be the interior of the tapestry workshop of St Isabella, with the tapestry-makers intent on their work and with clients looking at a tapestry hung on the wall. In the eighteenth century the work was enlarged on all sides with several layers of restoration. In 1931 Hendy recognized the tapestry in the background as being a copy of the *Rape of Europa* by Titian, already in the Prado, and also copied by Rubens (now in the Gardner Museum, Boston). The work is of uncertain date between 1647 and 1657. It was painted for Don Pedro de Arce, the king's huntsman, in whose inventory of 1667 it was already listed as *Fable of Arachne*. In 1725 it went into the royal collection with the title *Las Hilanderas* (*The Tapestry Weavers*), and was badly damaged in the fire at the Alcazar in 1734. Possibly the canvas was restored and enlarged after this. It has been in the Prado since 1819.

77-9 The Royal Family, c. 1656. Oil on canvas, 318 × 276 cm. Madrid, Prado. The alternative title, *Las Meninas* (*The Maids of Honour*), is taken from the two ladies who accompany the little Infanta Margarita, and was given to the painting in 1843. In 1666 it was already in the royal collection, and it has been in the Prado since 1819. An old copy belongs to Mr Ralph Bankes, of Kingston Lacy, Wimborne, Dorset, England.

TOMAS·

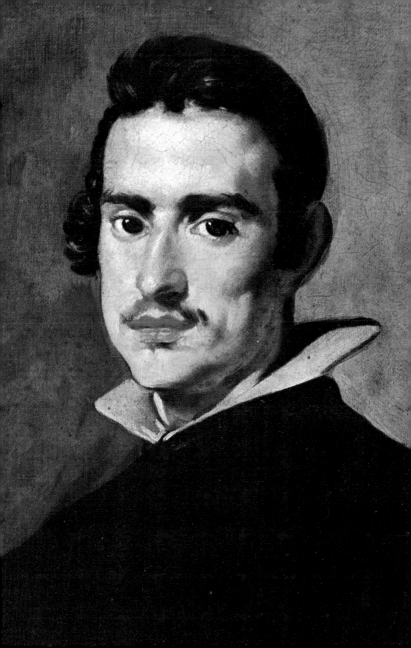

11

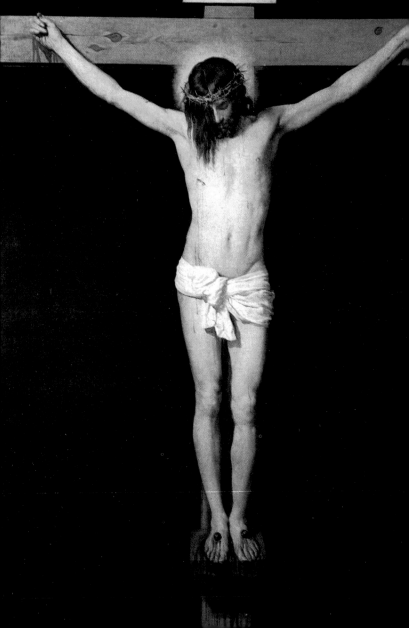

MOENIPPVS

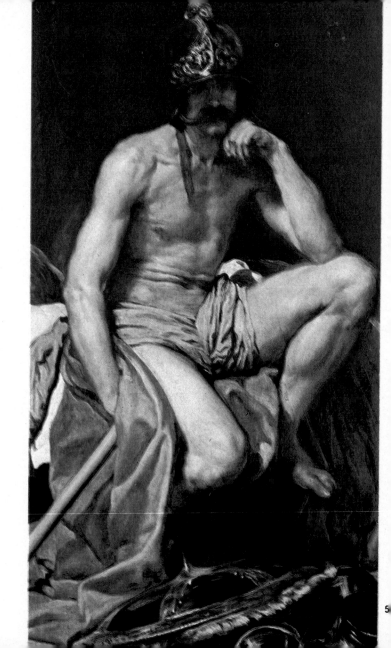

713.